EX LIBRIS

LEOPOLD CLASSIC LIBRARY

PLINY THE YOUNGER & FRANCO MOROLI

LETTERS TO CORNELIUS TACITUS ON THE DEATH OF THE ELDER PLINY AND THE ERUPTION OF VESUVIUS, A.D. 79 : A NEW VERSION

LEOPOLD CLASSIC LIBRARY

Published by Leopold Classic Library

This book is sold subject to the condition that it shall not, by way of trade or otherwise, be lent, re-sold, hired out, or otherwise circulated without the publisher's prior consent in any form or binding or cover other than that in which it is published and without a similar condition including this condition being imposed on the subsequent purchaser.

All rights reserved

This book has been printed 'on demand' from the Leopold Classic Library, and is therefore environmentally sustainable. There is no wastage from excessive or unnecessary printing, nor any energy wasted in pulping unsold copies.

www.leopoldclassiclibrary.com

Leopold Classic Library is delighted to publish this classic book as part of our extensive collection. As part of our on-going commitment to delivering value to the reader, we have also provided you with a link to a website, where you may download a colour PDF version of this work for free.

Free download of the colour PDF available here:
http://tinyurl.com/leopold-letterstocorneli00plinrich

Many of the books in our collection have been out of print for decades, and therefore have not been accessible to the general public. Whilst the books in this collection have not been hand curated, an aim of our publishing program is to facilitate rapid access to this vast reservoir of literature. As a result of this book being first published many decades ago, it may have occasional imperfections. These imperfections may include poor picture quality, blurred or missing text. While some of these imperfections may have appeared in the original work, others may have resulted from the scanning process that has been applied. However, our view is that this is a significant literary work, which deserves to be brought back into print after many decades. While some publishers have applied optical character recognition (OCR), this approach has its own drawbacks, which include formatting errors, misspelt words, or the presence of inappropriate characters. Our philosophy has been guided by a desire to provide the reader with an experience that is as close as possible to ownership of the original work. We hope that you will enjoy this wonderful classic book, and that the occasional imperfection that it might contain will not detract from the experience.

LETTERS TO CORNELIUS TACITUS ON THE DEATH OF THE ELDER PLINY AND THE ERUPTION OF VESUVIUS, A.D. 79 : A NEW VERSION

PLINY THE YOUNGER

LETTERS
TO CORNELIUS TACITUS

ON THE DEATH OF THE ELDER PLINY
AND THE ERUPTION OF VESUVIUS A. D. 79

A NEW VERSION

PRIVATELY PRINTED BY
MOROLI'S TRAVEL BUREAU

ROME   NAPLES
77-78, VIA DEL TRITONE   11 & 15, VIA DOMENICO MORELLI

Gift of
Harry East Miller

PREFACE.

The city of Pompei, originally a settlement of Greek colonists, as almost all the cities on the charming coast of Campania had been, was at the time of its destruction mainly Roman. Grecian civilization however was in every way manifest as it was conspicuously evident by the gracefulness of the buildings which were essentially Greek in style.

The city had been greatly damaged by an earthquake, A. D. 63, which apparently destroyed the principal buildings; certainly it had overthrown the dwelling houses which during the following sixteen years had either been rebuilt or were in process of rebuilding. This earthquake must have had some connection with Vesuvius, the volcanic forces of which, during that period, were working and so terribly let loose in the year A. D. 79.

The Second Letter of Pliny the Younger to Cornelius Tacitus clearly alludes to convulsive movements of the earth for several days immediately preceding the eruption, and we may infer from this that manifestations of the activity of Mount Somma

Gift of
Harry East Miller

UNIV. OF
CALIFORNIA

PREFACE.

The city of Pompei, originally a settlement of Greek colonists, as almost all the cities on the charming coast of Campania had been, was at the time of its destruction mainly Roman. Grecian civilization however was in every way manifest as it was conspicuously evident by the gracefulness of the buildings which were essentially Greek in style.

The city had been greatly damaged by an earthquake, A. D. 63, which apparently destroyed the principal buildings; certainly it had overthrown the dwelling houses which during the following sixteen years had either been rebuilt or were in process of rebuilding. This earthquake must have had some connection with Vesuvius, the volcanic forces of which, during that period, were working and so terribly let loose in the year A. D. 79.

The Second Letter of Pliny the Younger to Cornelius Tacitus clearly alludes to convulsive movements of the earth for several days immediately preceding the eruption, and we may infer from this that manifestations of the activity of Mount Somma must also have been evident, and that the populations of the district were already in a state of alarm when the great explosion took place August 23-27, A. D 79. There is no doubt therefore that most of the inhabitants, bearing in mind the effects of the catastrophe of 63 A. D., must have been terrified at the first indications of the impending peril of an eruption or of a new earthquake, and must have fled from the city carrying with them everything of their portable treasures and goods; the very limited number of bodies found in the excavations would bear out this theory. But whither did they flee?

Though we learn from various writers that the exodus of the people was towards the sea, we must conjecture that as there were no means of escape in that direction for want of boats, and because the winds " were blowing dead on shore „, " the water was greatly agitated and the waves running high „, caused even Pliny to remain on shore. Nor can we admit that they fled towards Naples, for then they would incur a greater peril by going round the burning mountain and towards the streams of lava which flowed over Herculanum. It would seem therefore that the only way of escape was across the level plain towards Salerno and Paestum, the ancient Poseidonia.

For seventeen centuries the city remained buried and neglected to the extent that the site itself had been forgotten, and it was only by a fortuitous combination that it was discovered and identified in the XVIII. century, as it was also the case with Herculanum which lay under the modern city of

Resina and was accidentally found during the digging of a well.

The excavations done up to 1912 were not carried out on scientific principles. The thought of identifying the houses was second to that of finding treasures which, being scattered over the world in galleries and private collections, attest the absolute lack of the spirit of preservation or reconstruction. Little consideration as well was given to the study of the actual events of the catastrophe, or of the destiny of the city after the great eruption.

Thus we have been deprived of serious critical studies as to the life of the pompeians, their social development and culture which could have been the result of greater accuracy in excavating the ruined city, in reconstructing the edifices and in taking greater care of their preservation. Even at the present day - what would seem incredible in a country so jealous and proud of its glorious past as Italy is- great monuments such as the House of the Vettii, are left with their magnificent wall paintings and decorations exposed to the deteriorating effects of the sun, rain and cold weather in such a way that the wonderful frescoes may soon fade away and be lost to the enjoyment of lovers of Art and History.

But was the city of Pompei utterly entombed in the year 79 A. D., and did its name and site wane suddenly from the memory of men? Though History is silent on this point, there seems to be no doubt that the ruined state of the buildings, and the fright of the survivors, prevented every idea of repair or reconstruction at the time. However the recent excavations, conducted under the very praiseworthy scientific methods employed by Prof. Vittorio Spinazzola, have revealed the fact that valuables and effects were missing everywhere, and that the survivors must have returned, dug out the cinders and searched the houses, exporting valuables as they found them, which fact enables us to conclude that parts of the buildings were still uncovered and visible, so as to be identified after the awful catastrophe, and that only subsequent eruptions completed the enshrouding process.

These few notes will enable the visitor to have a clear idea of the events connected with the terrible occurrence; for the rest the word is given to Pliny the Younger, the elegant writer who has painted in immortal colours the scenes of the great tragedy that after eighteen centuries still attracts the attention and stirs the sentiment of humanity.

The new excavations, this magnificent work of reconstruction and identification, which enable us to grasp a glimpse of palpitating social life in the first century of the Christian Era, are indeed one of the most salient and most genial accomplishments in the history of modern archaeology. Let us hope that the new excavations may be continued with the same genial scientific methods and purposes heretofore employed so that still new revelations of the Art and social development of our Ancestors may be rendered possible.

Franco Moroli.

LETTERS
TO CORNELIUS TACITUS

LETTER XVI. — *Pliny the Younger to Cornelius Tacitus.*

As you ask me to give you an account of my Uncle's death, so that you may hand down to posterity an exact relation of it, and of the awful disaster that occasioned it, I now comply with your request, which deserves my acknowledgment; for if in your writings you commemorate the fatality, it will be rendered famous, and my Uncle's name will be for ever illustrious.

Having lost his life in the fearful catastrophe which destroyed and laid waste many towns and villas on the coast of a most charming country, which, it seems to me, should promise him an everlasting memorial, and although my Uncle himself has written many imperishable works, yet I am fully persuaded that the mention of him in your immortal writings will render his name for ever renowned.

II.

I esteem happy those persons to whom the gods have bestowed the gift of doing actions, like his, worthy of being related, or of relating them in a manner worthy of reading. Still happier are they who are possessed of both of these talents, and in the van of such persons my Uncle may justly be placed as his own works and your history will fully prove. Indeed I should have written to you an account of the disaster, even if you had not requested me.

My Uncle was in command of the naval fleet at Misenum. On the 23rd. of August A. D. 79, about one o'clock in the afternoon, my mother drew his attention to a cloud extraordinary in size and shape. He had taken a rest for a while in the sun, as his habit was, and had just had a drink of fresh water, having thrown himself on a couch where he was studying. At my mother's call he rose and ascended a slight eminence from where he could observe this phenomenon better. It was difficult to distinguish, in the distance, from where the cloud was rising, but it afterwards appeared clearly that it was from Vesuvius.

To describe its appearance exactly I cannot do better than to liken it to a pine tree rising to a great height and spreading out, as it were, into great branches, by a sudden gust of air which impelled it upward at first, causing it to expand, and then to decrease by the pressure of its own weight. At times it appeared of a white colour, and again dark and spotted, changing colours according as it was impregnated with earth or cinders.

This extraordinary prodigy surprised my Uncle,

III.

and as he was a man of learning, he decided to investigate it. For this purpose he ordered a boat to put to sea at once, and gave me leave to accompany him if I wished.

However as he had given me something to write out, I replied I would rather stay and keep to my studies.

As he was leaving the house, carrying his tablets with him, he received a note from the wife of Bassus whose villa was at Rectina (1) at the foot of the mountain, entreating him to come to their rescue, as they were greatly frightened, and seemed to see no way of escape but by sea. My uncle thereupon changed his intention, and what he first desired to do only for scientific purposes he now determined to perform under a noble and altruistic impulse. He therefore ordered the galleys to put to sea purposing to go to the aid not only of Rectina, but also of the numerous towns along that beautiful coast. He hastened to the spot from which everyone was fleeing, and he steered his course to where the danger seemed greatest. Calmly and with great presence of mind he made and dictated his observations on the phenomena of that dreadful scene. He approached so close to the mountain that the ashes and cinders which were becoming each moment thicker and hotter fell into the ships, and not only these but also pumice stone and pieces of burning rock. The danger now was of the ships going a-ground by sudden retreats of the sea, and they were in péril likewise from the huge masses that came down from the mountain, and prevented those on shore to embark. He was now undecided whether to continue or to return to Misenum, but the pilot said to him "Fortune favours the brave, let us go to where Pomponianus is „. Pomponianus' residential place was then at Stabiae, a town on the shore, separated by a bay formed by the sinuosity of the land. My Uncle then put farther out to sea as soon as the wind was favourable, and although not in actual danger for the moment, yet he deemed this advisable as the wind was blowing dead on shore, and might increase. As he had already sent his baggage on board, he was able to reach Pomponianus whom he found in a state of great alarm. He encouraged him not to give way to fright, and more effectually to calm his fears, he himself appeared unconcerned and ordered a bath to be prepared, then, having bathed, he sat down to supper affecting a cheerfulness which, if not real, was at least heroic,

Immense flames now expanded from Vesuvius which the darkness of the night rendered bright and luminous. To allay the apprehensions of his friends he assured them that those flames were caused by the burning villages that had been abandoned by the inhabitants who had fled.

He then retired to rest and slept soundly, thus clearly showing what little apprehension of danger he had, and his breathing being heavy and sonorous on account of his corpulence, was heard by the attendants waiting without. As the court was beginning to be filled with stones and ashes, it was necessary to waken

V.

him, for if he remained longer it would have been impossible for him to get out. He accordingly arose and sought Pomponianus and the others who had been too anxious to think of sleep. They instantly held a consultation as to whether it would be better to trust to the protection of the houses which now rocked more and more frequently as if violently shaken from the very foundation; or to seek the open country where however the calcined stones and burning cinders, though light, were falling in constant showers threatening destruction to everything. At last it was resolved to attempt the open fields, to which all hurriedly agreed, and my Uncle on calm reflection adopted it. They all then tied pillows and napkins on their heads as a protection, with no other defence against the showers of stones that were falling.

It was now day, but the darkness was thicker than the darkest night, and was relieved only by torches and other lights. It was decided to go further along the sea-shore and see if it would be safe to go on board the ships, but this was found impossible as the water was greatly agitated and the waves running high, conseguently they all decided to remain temporarily on shore. A sail cloth was then spread for my Uncle who lay down upon it, and called twice for cold water which was given him. He was however immediately obliged to rise, for the flames causing a strong whiff of sulphur had dispersed the party. Assisted by two of his attendants he raised himself from the ground but instantly fell down dead, suffocated, I believe, by the noxious vapours, as He

VI.

had always been afflicted with a weak throat which at times was inflamed. For three days the darkness continued when, as soon as it was light, his body was found intact and uninjured, in the same dress which he had worn when he fell, and he looked as if sleeping.

During all this time my mother and I remained at Misenum. But as this has no connection with your history, and as you merely requested particulars of my Uncle's death, I will conclude here, simply adding that I have faithfully related to you what I ~~have~~ myself have been either an eye witness of, or received notice of immediately after the sad event, and before there was time to vary the truth.

You will therefore cull out of this whatever may be useful to you as a historian; for writing a letter to a friend is one thing, and writing a historical event for the public is another. Adieu.

(I) There is some uncertainty in ancient manuscripts and also in printed editions on the reading of this passage. The name of Rectina is generally taken as being that of the wife of Bassus. However we are of the opinion that Rectina is the name of a town which most likely stood in the immediate vicinity of Herculanum, from which is probably derived the modern name of Resina, a town built on the buried city of Herculanum. This theory seems to us to be supported by the passage immediately following, which reads: " He therefore ordered the galleys to put to sea purposing to go to the aid not only of Rectina but also of the numerous towns along that beautiful coast „ which leaves no doubt that the author alluded to a town and not to a person.

VII.

LETTER XX. — *Pliny the Younger to Cornelius Tacitus.*

It seems that the letter I wrote to you at your request, concerning my Uncle's death, has awakened in you a desire to know something of the terrors and dangers which I suffered while I remained at Misenum, for I believe my narrative ended there.

" Though my soul recoils with horror, my tongue shall tell the story „ (I).

When my Uncle left us I spent some time at my studies which indeed had been my reason for staying behind, till it was time to take my bath.....

For some days previous there had been frequent shocks of earthquake, but this not being unusual in Campania, did not alarm us very much. However the shocks on that night, August 23. A. D. 79, were so violent that they actually overturned everything around us. I was about to awaken my mother when she rushed into my room; we left the house and sat in the open court which occupied a space between the building and the sea. As I was then eighteen years old, I know not whether to call my behaviour at this critical juncture temerity or folly, but I occupied myself in reading Livy, even making extracts from that author, as if nothing serious was happening around. Just at this instant we received a visit from a friend of my Uncle's, who had lately returned from Spain, and he, seeing me engaged in reading, as I sat with my mother, reproved her for her calm demeanour, and me for my heedless unconcern; but I continued my reading. The morning dawned with a feeble light; the houses tottered around us, and though we were on open ground, the place was so restricted that it was unsafe to remain there any longer as we were in imminent danger, and so decided to get away from the town. We were followed by a crowd of panic-stricken people, and as to a terror smitten mind the suggestion of another is always better than its own, they pressed upon us so closely as to impel us onwards on the road. When we got a convenient distance from the buildings we stood still in the midst of a most dangerous and fearful scene. The vehicles we had ordered to be drawn up, were swayed backwards and forwards, though on level ground, nor could we stay them, even when we tried to do so with great stones. The waves of the sea rolled back on themselves and seemed driven from the shore by the convulsive motion of the earth; the water had receded from the land, leaving dead fishes on the shore. On the land side a black and ominous cloud in which every now and then were zig-zag flashes of light, showed behind it masses of flame like sheet lightning but much larger.

Upon this our Spanish friend, whom I mentioned above, energetically urged my mother and me to get away saying, " If your uncle be safe, certainly he wishes you to be in safety too, but if he has perished, no doubt he desired that you should not; why do you delay to escape? We replied that we could never think of our own safety while we were uncertain as to his. Upon this our friend left us in great haste to escape from danger.

The cloud which had already enshrouded Misenum and the island of Capri now began to descend and spread itself over the sea. My mother urged and begged, even commanded me to make my escape, saying that I was young and could easily get away from danger; as for herself, escape was impossible on account of her age and corpulency; and she added that she could willingly meet death if she knew that she was not the occasion of mine. Not only did I absolutely refuse to leave her, but taking her by the hand I compelled her to go with me. She complied reluctantly, reproaching herself as being the cause of my delaying to escape.

The ashes were still falling on us but not very heavily. I looked back and saw behind us a dense black cloud that seemed to follow us, as it spread itself over the land. " Let us get away from the high road „, I said, " while we can see before us, for if we should fall on the road we should be trodden over to death in the darkness by the crowd behind us „.

Night fell soon, not such a night as when the sky is clouded and there is no moon, but that of a closely-shut room where no light is burning.

The lamentations of women, the wailing of children, and the shouts and blasphemies of men echoed around us in the darkness; women calling their children, all crying aloud for their relatives and friends, endeavouring to recognize each other by their voices;

some bewailing their own fate; others calling on death to deliver them while they were in terror of death, and some invoking the gods to aid them, the majority being convinced that there were no gods, and that the end of the world, of which they had heard, had come.

There were some who increased the terror of others by imaginary or wilful exaggerations, by declaring that Misenum was on fire and partly destroyed and their exaggerations found credence with the terrorized people.

The atmosphere now became clearer but it seemed that this was only the presage of approaching flames rather than the dawn of morning, and it proved so. Again gross darkness enshrouded us, while the fire fell, though at some distance from us, but a heavy shower of ashes rained upon us which we were obliged continually to shake off, or else we should be entirely covered with them and crushed to death. I might boast that not a sigh, nor an expression of fear escaped me during the whole of that terrible scene, as I felt the miserable yet over-powering consolation that in this terrible calamity I was perishing with the world itself.

Day broke at last, and the darkness gradually disappeared; the sun gave a feeble light as if in partial eclipse, and we saw every object around covered with ashes as if changed by a fall of snow hiding the landscape from our view. We now returned to Misenum and refreshed ourselves as well as we could, but we passed a most anxious night between hope

XI.

and fear; for the earthquake shocks still continued, while many persons, maddened by fear, ran wildly about, increasing their own terror and that of others by foolish prognostications. Notwithstanding the danger my mother and I had passed, and which still threatened us, we decided to remain where we were till we could get tidings of my Uncle.

You will read this account without any idea of inserting it in your history, an honour it does not merit, and in truth you must attribute it to your own request, as it seems not worth even the trouble of a letter. Adieu.

(I) Virgil, Æneid, Book; v. 11.

Printed in Great
Britain
by Amazon